TWELVE ROMAN THRESHOLDS

TWELVE ROMAN THRESHOLDS

A Structural History of Rome in Twelve Poems
by J. A. Gucci

Pressure System Press
New York, New York

2026

Twelve Roman Thresholds: A Structural History of Rome in Twelve Poems
© 2026 J. A. Gucci

This book was composed according to the principles of Absolute Composition, a method of structural poetry based on one-to-one correspondence between natural systems and conceptual triads.

Epigraphs are drawn from classical sources in the public domain. Translations have been adapted where necessary for clarity and brevity.

Printed in the United States of America

First Edition

ISBN: 978-1-972788-07-3

www.jagucci.com

CONTENTS

How to Use This Book

Each page contains a short poem.

You are not being asked to interpret it in the usual
way.
Instead, focus on what is happening.

Look closely at the details.
Notice movement, interaction, and change.

Look for:

- what condition is present
- what interacts or responds
- what emerges from that interaction

Each poem corresponds to a system from ancient
Greece.
As you read, try to identify how the system works.

Do not ask what the poem means.
Ask what the system does.

The goal is not to explain the poem, but to
recognize the pattern.

As you move through the book, notice how
different parts connect and influence one another.
Each system forms through interaction.

*"The Senate is the belly, but the Plebs are the limbs.
Without the limbs, the belly starves."*
—Menenius Agrippa

Stunted Willow Shoots

Stunted willow shoots—
fatted calf nibbling,
browsing—
terminal buds.

Gnarled woody nubs
buried in snow,
wide shallow river—
frozen fish.

Grey wolves
howl—
herds of fawn
scuttle—

water sprouts.

"Veni, vidi, vici."
—*Julius Caesar*

Cirques

Snow over ice—
granular,
packed—
over peak.

Flow—
grinding and plucking,
polishing—

cirque.

"All roads lead to Rome."
—Publius Papinius Statius

Taproot

Tapered—
trunk to tip—
firm,
supple.

Surging sap—
water,
looming green
canopy—

wind waft—
uproot.

"The rich swallowed up the small farms."
— Plutarch

Hardpan

Crumbling clumps—
moist,
clew—
boring burrows.

Harvest—
hard-packed
sand,
yellow leaves—

landslide.

"The authority of those who teach is often an obstacle to those who wish to learn."
—Cicero

Murmuration

Starlings in a swarm—
seven,
nestled in the core.

Hawk screech—
undulating streaks
peaks
pulsing spheres—

carrion.

"The more corrupt the state, the more numerous the laws." — Tacitus

Cutbank

Eddies—
vertical swirls—
meandering river.

Silt rapids
bars—

cut banks—
cattails.

"With such an array of indispensable structures carrying so many waters, compare if you will the idle pyramids."
—Frontinus

Aquifer

Rain—
fossil water,

squeezed
cracked bed—

well—
spring.

"Victory breeds hatred."
—Livy

Caldera

Hot rock
buoyant in a chamber—
sticky
surging bubbles
shatter—

pumice plumes—
ash,
empty throat—

caldera.

"They are slaves? No, they are men."
—*Seneca*

24

Dulosis

Sickle—
propaganda pheromones.

Cocoons—
twitching in a tunnel.

Hatched—
a worker forages—
heaps of grain,
mounds of seed—

dead parasite.

"In peace there is nothing so becoming to a man as modesty and humility; but when war breaks out he must act like a savage beast."
—Tacitus

Rift

Cracked crust
yanked—

cool crust—
seaward—

wall.

"After his death, they decreed him a god."
—*Suetonius*

Neutron Star

Dust cloud—
squeezed,
red glow—

falling inward,
melding,
sun—

quenched—
blue-white—

pulsing.

"They make a desert and call it peace."
—Tacitus

Ghost Pipe

Solid green
black,
canopy under sun.

Ghost pipe—
dark forest floor—

Jackstraw—
canker bloom—

snag forest.

Appendix

Structural Thresholds and System Limits

This appendix does not explain the poems.
It defines the conditions under which they operate.

1. The Threshold Principle

Each poem models a system approaching a limit.

A condition builds.
A force intensifies.
A boundary is reached.

At that boundary, the system changes.

This is the threshold.

2. Three Structural Phases

Every poem operates through three phases:

- Accumulation — growth, expansion, pressure
- Strain — instability, imbalance, saturation
- Release — collapse, rupture, transformation

These phases may not appear in order.
But they are always present.

3. Compression and Scale

Roman systems expand beyond local balance.

They:

- Extend across distance
- Increase in density
- Multiply connections

As scale increases, so does pressure.

Thresholds emerge from excess.

4. Points of Failure

A threshold is not gradual.

It is a point where:

- A structure can no longer sustain itself
- A force exceeds containment
- A system reorganizes or breaks

Failure is not an accident.

It is structural.

5. Domains of Pressure

Each poem draws from systems under stress:

- Geological (rift, caldera, compression)
- Hydrological (cutbanks, aquifers, erosion)
- Biological (parasitism, overgrowth, collapse)
- Astronomical (gravitational compression, implosion)

These are not metaphors for Rome.

They are systems that behave like it.

6. Roman Correspondence

Each system parallels a structural condition in
Roman civilization:

- Expansion beyond sustainable limits
- Centralization under increasing strain
- Resource extraction and redistribution
- Internal pressure leading to rupture

Rome does not simply grow.

It accumulates until it must transform.

7. Irreversibility

Unlike earlier volumes:

- Egypt stabilizes
- Greece interacts

Rome crosses thresholds.

After a threshold is reached:

The system does not return to its previous state.

8. Reader Function

You are not identifying meaning.

You are identifying:

- Where pressure builds
- Where the system destabilizes
- Where the threshold is crossed
-

The poem ends near or at that moment.

You must recognize it.

9. Series Position

Within the Twelve series:

- Egypt — sustained systems
- Greece — interacting systems
- Rome — systems under pressure
- Medieval — systems at transition

Each volume isolates a different structural condition.

10. Final Condition

If the poem feels like it is about to break, it is working.

Rome is not defined by what it builds.

It is defined by what it pushes
to the point of no return.

The Twelve Series

Each book in this series presents systems through short, structured poems.

Rather than describing events, the poems model how systems form, interact, and change over time.

Each volume focuses on a different civilization, using the same method to reveal how complex societies develop.

History

Mesopotamia — Formation
Greece — Interaction
Rome — Expansion and Collapse
Medieval — Thresholds

Creative Writing

Twelve Small Windows
Twelve Loops
Twelve Mirrors
Twelve Rooms

Philosophy

Twelve Iron Paradoxes

About the Author

J. A. Gucci is an educator and writer whose work focuses on systems, structure, and the relationship between form and meaning.

His books present historical and conceptual material through short, structured poems designed to model how systems form and change over time.

Colophon

This book was set in a clear, readable typeface to
support careful observation and sustained
attention.

The poems follow a consistent structure to
emphasize interaction, response, and the
emergence of patterns.

Designed and produced as part of the Twelve
series.